I DON'T KNOW HOW THAT HAPPPENED

I DON'T KNOW HOW THAT HAPPENED

OLIVER DRISCOLL

RECENT WORK PRESS

I don't know how that happened
Recent Work Press
Canberra, Australia

Copyright © Oliver Driscoll, 2020

ISBN: 9780648685364 (paperback)

 A catalogue record for this book is available from the National Library of Australia

All rights reserved. This book is copyright. Except for private study, research, criticism or reviews as permitted under the Copyright Act, no part of this book may be reproduced, stored in a retrieval system, or transmitted in any form by any means without prior written permission. Enquiries should be addressed to the publisher.

Cover image: Stephane Mingot on unsplash
Cover design: Recent Work Press
Set by Recent Work Press

recentworkpress.com
SS

For Jess

Contents

A flat door in a flat wall	1
How good it was	5
And then	10
Six weeks	12
You and me x	14
Where's the fun	16
Suddenly	18
One of several attractions	20
A pattern language	22
September	23
'Keep it.'	26
Strange fruit	27
Both sides	28
Outdtoors #11	31
Lines for a film #8	33
Table #6	35
Bedroom #4	37
Sway forward, step back	39
Leaving the north	41
Economy	44
Unsettled and	46
A Second Child	48
Lines for a poem # 7	49
Not feeling like myself	54
More to the point	55
New in the family	58
Afterword	62

A flat door in a flat wall

After I cleaned the fridge, I cleaned the stove.

Wash your feet, she said, with disdain.

I answered my phone.

I put milk in my coffee.

I hung up my phone when I got to the gate of our apartment building. There were people who didn't live in the block standing on the grass between the fence and the building, where people never stand. The auction at number eleven would soon get started. I thought, I may as well see what another of these apartments looks like.

I told Tim from upstairs that I was having trouble centring the clay on the wheel and he said, you said that months ago.

I texted Tim to say, your shower is dripping.

Katie texted to say, but you guys are just such light sleepers.

I replied, I think so, maybe.

During the auction, I stood in the corridor watching the auctioneer through the doorway. The rental tenant sat on the couch facing me. He seemed so happy to have so many people and so much happening in his apartment. A woman in a camel-coloured coat beside me said to a man with a clipboard, no, I'm not going to bid yet. The man was holding a box of chocolates to give to her if and when she did bid. She said, okay, ten, as in ten thousand more than the previous bid, but, she said, I don't want chocolates. You have to, the man said, someone will want them.

When the auction finished we all rushed out. As I went down the stairs I thought, suddenly the only people left in the apartment will be the woman in the camel coat, who had won, the auctioneers and the owner, who had been waiting in the kitchen, at the other end of the corridor. I wondered if the tenant would stay or leave. I didn't see him on the stairs.

There was a foosball table at the bottom of the stairs, beside the door.

The woman, I thought, had slowed the momentum of the auction in the way certain tennis players would slow a match when their opponent had the upper hand. I thought, to be a person who could slow things down.

Our apartment was off another stairway further down the block. In our entryway, Margaret from number seven, who was on her way out, said mournfully that lately her daughter had been shutting herself in her room and playing sad Spanish music. I said, I feel as though I've heard it playing. Putting her hands on my shoulders she said, I just feel like hugging you.

I pulled the metal drainage hole cover out from the bath and thought, I must fix it in place with silicone. I was worried about the rim rusting away. I unscrewed the front of the hot tap of the shower and when the handle came away the spring from within shot out towards me, and then momentarily caught on my shirt before falling into the bath and rolling into the open hole. I stepped into the bath, lowered myself onto my knees and looked into the plug hole, but I couldn't see the spring. I closed my eyes and tried to remember why I had been taking the handle off.

A kitchen fitter who had recently relocated from Macedonia moved into the front apartment. He said, I saw that chair you were working on. It's nice. You could sell them. If you need to borrow any tools, he said, I have many tools. A ladder, anything. Three or four weeks later he said, you know everything that happens in the building, and walked away.

Tim moved out. While I washed clay off my arms, Katie said to me, yeah, he drinks all the time. He's kind of violent. Katie was a dentist. I tried to picture Tim with a drink in his hands. I tried to picture him being violent. I tried to picture Katie standing over a patient with their mouth open.

Laura came over and I showed her the lights that we'd brought back from Japan. I pointed to the two hooked-together timber spheres that the cord ran through to enable the height to be adjusted, and said that we'd taken the detail from a Kunio Maekawa house. I told Laura about the man from Macedonia and said, this is the third time a man has moved in who was initially friendly but would later walk by me without saying anything. By the time he moved out, I said, the American man who lived in the front apartment before the Macedonian would talk to his dog about me as I passed but would never say anything directly to me. I said, I don't know if it's them or me. Laura said that a standup comic she'd watched a few nights earlier on Netflix had said that men are always, in some way, in a state of readiness to kill each other. What do you think, she said, kinda true, right? I asked her if she felt like eating and she said yes and I turned off the Japanese lights.

The cream-coloured garage floor has an oil stain in the corner. There's a bookshelf full of DVDs along the back wall. Some of the spines of the DVDs are blue, some are white.

How good it was

Rachel texted to say that the crane from behind had fallen on the skinny neighbouring house pulling much of it down but missing ours entirely so she was fine.

●

There was something in the yard, she wrote, that she'd thought had been thrown from the house but it was only the ice cream container full of soil that I had left out there months ago. I didn't think it had been months.

●

She'd then written, *I'm in the living room*, as though I was in the next room and she was speaking rather than texting. I wondered if she'd been shaking as she typed into her phone.

●

This kind of thing, I thought, never happened to us. I didn't know why it never did. I didn't know if this was something I wanted, something that could be good for us.

●

The crane had been parked there for as long as we'd lived in the house. It was thick metal and neither seemed in or out of place but there was something upsetting about the way it was hunched over. Unlike the trees, it was bright insect green. I'd wanted to not look at it.

•

I wanted the crane to make a sound but it never did.

•

Reading Rachel's texts, I'd imagined scattered plastic toys and lunch boxes.

•

No, I remembered, an elderly man had lived there but had moved out with the help of a young woman who had introduced herself to Rachel. I had only seen the man and the woman remove bags and suitcases.

•

The house had seemed to be uninhabited since then. They'd left a wooden broom lying across his driveway. They've swept their way out, Rachel had said, pointing at the broom.

•

I tried to recall what the woman had looked like but all I could see was her square dress, and large cold-looking hands that may have belonged to the man. Perhaps, I thought, they'd had similar hands.

•

Rachel texted again to say she'd forgotten the crane was even around.

•

I thought of Rachel saying *that's the difference between you and me*, and then, days or weeks later, *that's the difference between your family and mine*, though I can't remember what those differences were.

•

It's hard to tell where sound comes from around there, with the big blue radiata pines.

•

I'd thought of walking up his driveway or jumping the fence to

•

look through the man's windows to see what furniture had been left behind. It was

- probably from the 60s.

- The question of how then to have gotten in, and

- what to have done with it.

- He wouldn't have known how good it was.

I watch out my window as a man in a lime-green polo shirt lets air out of the tyres of a child's bicycle that's upside down on the driveway of the neighbouring apartment building. He squishes the flat tyres with his hands, both at the same time. He then picks up a small hand pump and pumps up the front tyre and then the back tyre. When he's done, he places the pump on the concrete driveway and stands up straight. I can see that he's panting. He lifts his arms above his head and then looks towards me. I don't know if he can see me. I try to remain still. He then puts his hands on his hips and swings his torso one way and then the other.

And then

And then, with such immediacy, we flee, with drummed-in speed, all of us, a broken wave, And then, for months, the field is green with footprints.

The door between the garage and the house is the same as the doors within the house, with four inset panels. The door looks out of place from the garage side but alright from inside.

Six weeks

Six weeks
ago a friend's child told me
to write a list of the things
that are bigger than I am.
I said there are lots
of things. I took a biro
out of my pocket and wrote
down starvation, which
I thought was too clever,
too the kind of thing you
would say to a child. I said,
I'm not really in the mood, or,
I'm really not in the mood. I said,
I'd been on a plane. He
ran out from the room with his arms out
flat and straight and returned, too quickly,
wearing a cowboy hat, vest and holster.
So,
I thought, he's going
to shoot me. Instead, holding
the white pistol by the thin barrel, he
handed it to me and said, you
shoot me. I asked him why he'd put
on his machine voice. He said,
in the same way, it's an aeroplane voice. Where do I
shoot you, I asked. Umm
he said, putting a finger to his
forehead. No, he said, pointing at
his chest, here. The rest of the evening,
and week, and much of that
year went too quickly as well.

I chop one of the carrots one way and the other another way and ask myself which I prefer.

You and me x

You and me x
some funny kidwho
grabbed hammer and hit
Music to my ears
anger anger anger angeranger
he keeps hitting that note
when duringthe talk
she wrote down interstitial
It was so clean when we arrived
we'll never get it so clean again
I didn't think it was that clean
I shouldn't have had that
next time you'llknow
she's about ready to leave really leave
You could have done more
yes

While we stood waiting for a gap in the cars so we could cross the road, she said, let's be kind. I said, I wasn't sure about that shirt when you bought it, but now I like it.

Where's the fun

Cut-out magazine
Bodies, mouths and shapes.
Noiseless
We fumble or move about.
Every day a little less
Paper and more mouths.

He's the only person I know who says 'from now on'. I don't know how that happened.

Suddenly

In this way, months, years eluded
Identity. Themes, tendencies were consistently
Apprehended. Absently
Overlooked. What started with our
First born was continued, appropriated,
By our second.
                    A darling white-haired thing

I took three ten dollar notes out of my wallet to pay and then said, sorry, too many, and put one back.

One of several attractions

The same old nostalgia.
This was back when we were coming
Down into Ayo Ayo. The dull atmosphere
Assuming us like wet flour—our billboards cover
Three European languages—inch thick padding,
A lifeless wind. New guardrails. They sell
Fish out in the open. The very young and the very old
Alike seem to walk with a diagonal; a cavernous,
Scored-aluminium check-in. Nine
Visitors out of ten. The newly
Finished & the newly landed. The terminus
Of thought. Dampened. Obsolete. So we eddy
Around
The rain where the collar
Meets. Where the dollar is
Untouched. Where
One solid hour was a kind
Of gravelly meal: 'breathe
The good air.'
This is a watch,
A break in the tide. Agitated awake.
Still awake, still insufferable.
Never asleep. Never cold. Never
That soft subtext of humour.
'Breathe the good air.' (Breathe
The good air.)

I turn the door handle to open the door and think, I wonder how heavy the door handle is. I ask myself if it would be hollow or solid. Frankly, it could be either.

A pattern language

A friend who is married to another friend sends me a link to a photo of a house near trees on an architect's website.

They have two children chickens I don't know how many one or two cats it's been a while since I've seen them they live in Brisbane in a square house grow flowers food she was a florist he studied horticulture did drawings in pen she does laps in a pool.

But here at night pipes bang in the apartment above people walk push objects around it's cold it seems so nice there is, I think, such a distance between seeming and being or being and continuously being I don't know if I should worry about the chickens the cat or the cats the flowers the food.

I reply, it's just a weathered frame she says, I know, I want to live in a weathered frame.

I've always liked them I think I should worry don't worry enough I google paint stripper macbook pro.

September

Sand speaks with every step
does it always make this sound
at a loss
the trim fabric of purpose
has given up its shape
I cannot make memory incohere
or amount
We must

A man sits down in front of me and I think, for all I know he could have dice in his pockets. Or in more than one pocket.

But bakers have bad lungs too, she says.

'Keep it.'

The phone is ringing but I try to remember whether the line was 'those are the people who are important' or 'those are the people who were important' or whether it was something else again. Is it going to just keep ringing, I wonder. Another thing I don't know is who are the people she refers to, who are or were important. As night falls, the phone stops ringing and I look around for the book.

Strange fruit

Where are they from he said and I said Bolivia,
having just chopped the last of the branches
from the African tulip.

He is holding the saw, lifted it from the table.
I brought it in to demonstrate its bow, how it flaps and lashes,
this skeleton-thin black fish wanting its ocean.

Out in the yard, I kept thinking it would take part of me,
but not in exchange for the tree's limbs so much
as to feed its growing hunger, or simply because that's what it does:
reduce, remove, trim, leaving suture markings and nothing sealed.

Where will we hang our clothes now he said and I said we won't,
that we should have stopped doing that
years ago. Look at the coarsening of those trousers,
the blanched strips across your shirt.

Both sides

On the phone Melanie who I don't see often enough whose hair I've seen on facebook is now black says, but I don't know how you would feel about an *actual* living breathing child.

I think back to sitting across from her in a cafe with ribbed glass windows that we'd go to where the music was always too something even early in the morning and her then toddler pushing a skinned avocado half into the blue and yellow tabletop while she held the collapsed skin in her hand and said, he's learning to feed himself.

I remember once writing in a maths textbook, but I don't remember what I wrote.

A man on the television says, write a list, but I don't hear the rest of the sentence.

A very old friend I haven't seen in years says, Solitaire, which one was he? My friend, I think, sounds worn down. He says, I believe he was Greek. I don't know, I say.

A wildlife program I'm not really watching is naming the ten most patient animal species.

No, a woman says into her phone, evolution is far too slow.

I dig out the planter bed at the front of our apartment building and find a chunk of old concrete curved like gutter that someone has written into with their finger, TW heart TM.

During a media conference after the game, a basketball player I like says, but there's mystery everywhere.

There are three kinds of happiness.

I google 'evolution speed'.

Make a lasting impression.

Outdtoors #11

'Love is dead,'
she reads aloud,
turning to look quizzically
at her young father,
lying on the grass
reading a novel.
The words sprayed silver
on the jungle gym.

He says, he's that kind of guy, and I think, are they talking about me, and then I remember I don't know either of them, they are just people in the shop.

After he pays for his box of Monet postcards, he turns to the woman beside him and says, I've always liked impressionism.

Before hanging up, my father says, yeah but you could make a graph out of practically anything.

Lines for a film #8

Everyone is in a dizzy;
you must be observing;
that when you've been somnambulant for sixty
odd years; we cannot breathe
for the simple reason that the air
is not breathable; he's crisis fighting;
popping bubbles at my eye; when I
say bad it is horrible; two hours coming;
two hours going; saturated in no time;
for myself and for my prestige also;
there is no queue; or it will vanish
when the bus comes; I have no choice
but to succeed

It's so modern, says one of them. Yeah, I guess so, says the other, that hadn't crossed my mind. How many is too many, I ask. Don't think of it in those terms, he says.

Someone at work says she knows exactly what she would do if her partner were to come out as trans. I ask her if that's likely and she says no, but I'm not quick enough to think to ask her what she would do. Instead I say, do you know what you would do if he were to lose his mental capacity? Of course I do, she says.

I think, perhaps I should make a list.

Yeah, she says, so many people have done that to their hair. Don't take it too personally.

Table #6

Breathing space; to the north;
on the campus; in Manchuria;
all right in Prague;
the long night; Peking night;
breathing space; habits of thought;
the delegation trade; to the north;
living in open space;
the long night; different city;
the Hangchow below;
the world is eventful; one person's
breathing space;
holding the carpet down;
all right in Prague.

A plumber unblocking my bathroom sink says to me, people don't die in houses anymore.

Then the plumber says, if you're in an argument, always count one one thousand, two one thousand before replying. It takes some getting used to, he says, but it's worthwhile.

I suspect the man ordering coffee is a famous Canadian tennis player. It occurs to me that whenever I'm doing something, the famous Canadian tennis player is doing something else. This, I think, will be the closest we come to overlapping. I ask my friend how you ask a famous Canadian tennis player if they're a famous Canadian tennis player. He says, that sounds like a joke. But I don't know if he means it sounds like the setup or the punchline. I can't pinpoint how exactly, but I feel my friend and I have been at each other's throats all morning. I say to myself, this is just how it is with him. I don't feel comfortable enough to ask if what I said sounded like the setup or the punchline of a joke. Besides, I think, I've asked too many questions and it's up to me to make a statement now.

Bedroom #4

a white 42 point L
a scar beside my mum's
right eye from the book
I threw at her
aged 7
and mad.

I overhear her sister say, water on the bridge, and I think, if English wasn't her second language, I could use that.

Sway forward, step back

After 'Octofurcation' (extending Hokusai's The dream of the fisherman's wife*) by Antonia Pont*

I am dumb of my body.
This warm sodic field.
Enraged
by its coming uselessness.
End parts, unseen by me,
egg shaped, brittle and slow. I wish I could not.
If it's sex you speak of
what am I to give? I would
look through my things
scatter what I have
but I have nothing
but untrapped loping years
to boast about,
to hold above me
to make me so tall as
to scare and to attract.
How would you
like to elongate me?
How about now?
What I am saying
keep on asking of you
is that you forget all that
about fur and body and
segmentation. *This* bone
that troubles you, for the way
it moved through liquid to quieten
into *that* bone.
Leave it.
No, not like that. You are my master, yes,
but not like that.

My sister tells me about her boyfriend telling her about a phone call he received. I see him saying 'bring bring' and then pretending to answer a landline and saying, Johno here, in the particularly deep voice he uses on the phone. The next morning, having slept well and feeling fresh and awake, I think, he wouldn't have said 'bring bring'.

On a television panel, a man on the left side of politics who sometimes seems as though he belongs on the right says, what does your cat know of suffering? I realise I'm warming to him and think, you never know what's going to happen next.

During the tournament, some players grunt before they hit the ball, some while, and some after. With nothing in my closed hands, I try one after the other, but cannot time the swing, the cruising imaginary yellow ball, the grunt.

Leaving the north

Original 1980s imitation Ray-Bans, now rather gummy; 1993 city guide, signed by the fact-checker, a family friend; sweatbands, hardly worn; squash racket, never used; *Anthology of American Folk Music Volume Three* sleeve; clap sticks; didgeridoo, with native-bee nest, not suitable for playing; bag of frozen Christmas beetles; huntsman; puncture repair kit, suits bicycles, inflatables, camping equipment; pencil sketch of the goldfinch; celadon vase, works as an ice bucket; starfish; Vision Street Wear badge; sunscreen; bronze axe head, oxidising slightly.

Three bottles of ammonia; demineralised water; small pieces of metal, suit 1948 Skoda; three various-sized containers of nails and scalpels, not all rusted, suit small project; two-litre milk bottle of latex, hardly touched; star fruit tree with glass baubles, fits through most doors; Moreton Bay bugs; binoculars; darts; pendant lamp; aluminium clock radio; spare tyre; goggles; glass home distillery set; blue jeans, no buttons; buttons, no blue jeans; wool brush, with wool attached; fuse; heat lamp; musket.

Homemade Robin mask, shirt and cape; tarpaulin; trailer; rain-ruined hardcovers; moa bones; human skull; .35 and .18 Rotring pens, suit young architect; six kilograms of Lego, suit enthusiast or beginner; scratched women's tortoise-shell glasses, have only been used for driving; cast-iron moustaches; pencil sketch of a uterus; more moa bones; watermelon scoop; more bits of metal; dried citrus flowers; wooden train, in original box, suit child, or adult; Marsh Arab cufflinks; Goanna Oil.

Jumper leads; rasp; three drill bits; drill case; iron hand-painted British soldiers; *La Vie en Rose*; wire bust, found in bushes; two banana boards, found in bushes; pitching wedge, more like a five iron; spirit level; food processor, yellowing slightly; iron gate, found in bushes; assortment of WWII paratrooper badges; pink spray paint, suitable for road marking; gasmask; three knives, three forks

and two spoons with green-glass handles; five green-glass handles;
Birds of the East Coast.

I read an extract about a piece I wrote about Sarajevo and Bosnian literature at a small university panel event. At the end of the event, an audience member asked if I was of Bosnian heritage. No, I said. The man beside me on the panel said, ha, yeah, we used to be able to do that, right, claim other people's suffering. The piece is kind of about that, I said, how we see and think about other people's trauma.

Right, he said, as though he'd won something fair and square.

Economy

He
48 hours in Charles de Gaulle Airport
18 hours in Changi Airport
12 hours in the old Hong Kong airport
He
'Never see Hong Kong like that again.'
Never see Hong Kong like that again
Reading. Around.
The radio was always on
Crossing out entire pages
Wasted paragraphs, too many characters
An airport novel
Condensed into
Now Carver. Now...

I change the channel and then change it back and then I change it again and think, I could turn it off.

Unsettled and

Another time we entered the country
Had the effect of being.
We passed them again, drinking from a fountain
Across the southern border.
Had expected
The media had presented a heavy police presence.
That had dwindled
In the intervening weeks.
The years had the same
The effect of being cautioned.
In time, we grew accustomed
To the quiet and the generosity.
The walls were whitewashed
And we owned a cat.

I phone up about a chair on Gumtree. The seller says, you can't see it in the photos—there's only one photo, and it's dark and at an angle that doesn't seem to make sense—but the back isn't attached at the moment, it's just sitting there. Yeah, I thought so, I said. It should be super easy to fix, the man says cheerfully.

A Second Child

Patience
The door frame
Swollen air
The size of people
A cluster lamp
And working child
And take your time
To find your papers
A telephone rings
And quietens down
Patience, (the door frame)
And now we see her arm
A trampled glow
A dull remark
Mute from worthwhile pain
And quietens down
To dull remark

Lines for a poem # 7

When at last; clipped scoliosis of polished track; such a simple thing; cold; white; when I stood cold on the westbound platform (there alone / there with a dog / there with an older man / there with a younger man); when I, remiss; when at last he did alight; cold white; moguls of white to white snow; mountain folds; old linen; polished track;

When at last he did alight nothing so much as flickered; as moved; as waited; nothing so much as; when an open-topped train; white to white snow; this is where; this is where we waited; this is where the dog froze; this is where we left it; where we kicked the white snow over it and then away from it; white to white; cold; open-topped;

Tongues trussed and cluttered like wind; this is where the dog froze and this is where we left it; when at last he did alight; when eventually it muddied to midnight; cows, bricks, clipped scoliosis of polished track; this is a dog; this is a town in a medieval valley; it was such a simple thing; like ancient mountain folds; when the snow came sheltering down; nothing so much as; not yet choked by the blistering; when at last; this is an hour; and this is an hour;

A woman sitting two rows ahead of me and facing me on the tram says, you're like one of those confused kids who went to an international school and doesn't know which accent to use. I can't see the man she's speaking to because his head is hidden behind the head of another man. A moment later she says, again, you're like one of those confused kids who went to an international school and doesn't know which accent to use. I think, word for word. I wonder if her expression changes as she turns her head, or whether she only appears to have a different expression when seen side-on or front-on. I wonder if her expression is changing or if she appears to have a different expression depending on whether you see her from the side or from the front. As we turn a bend she says, pointing to something outside of the tram, 'free Syria'. A moment later she says, yeah, some graffiti said free Syria.

Earlier, as I walked down from Fitzroy into the city to catch the tram, I was talking to my partner on the phone about how the narrator in the novel I was reading at the time, and the narrator in a novel that was in some ways similar that I'd read a little while earlier, spoke about and navigated their own beauty and attractiveness. In the one I was reading at the time, I said, the narrator is seen as ugly at school and then beautiful at university, but either way, she's always surprised by how people react to her. But, I said, she was seen as ugly at school not because she was necessarily ugly but because they didn't know what to make of her. In the one I'd read earlier, I said, people found the narrator attractive, but she spoke as though she couldn't understand what it meant to be attractive. She could never understand the weight beauty had in any one situation, but she knew or felt it had a weight. My partner said, if you could be more beautiful, would you be? I don't know, I said, but I thought to myself, if either one of us was more attractive, it's unlikely we would be together. She said, there's something about this in books written by women, the strange access it gives. She then told me about a book by another woman in which the narrator does many things the author does. She said, for example, she rides a motorcycle. In the book, she said, the narrator keeps being brought into worlds because she's incredibly beautiful. But then, my partner said, I read in an interview that the author has always wished that she was more beautiful, that she can't help but feel she's been denied something. Would every interaction, my partner said, be subtly different in a way that would never enable you to say that this particular thing would not have otherwise been said or done?

I don't find the woman across from me on the tram attractive, I don't think, but I keep looking up at her. Her dress has a small bow under her throat, and just below that there's an opening. Her face is chubby and covered in freckles, like a kind of child's face you don't see anymore. At the next stop, the man concealing the head of the man beside her gets off. The man beside the woman with the bow just below her throat looks Middle Eastern. He's looking straight ahead but not at anything. He's wearing a cream-coloured button-up shirt and tan trousers. The cream-coloured shirt is too small for him and between each of the buttons I can see his chubby belly and chest, and I can see black hairs. She puts her face right up near his and his face softens and they stare at each other as though they are playing a game and then they kiss on the mouth very quickly and briefly. I look down at my book but then look up again and he's holding his phone. She says, she looks so much more grown up now, and then she says, how old is she?

The next time I look up he is staring ahead again, and again at nothing. And again she puts her face close to his and his face softens. I wonder how long they can keep doing that. The woman doesn't look directly at me, but I know she knows I'm watching them. I try to imagine the man jumping up, straightening his shirt and accusing me of looking at them, of wanting something from them. I think about how much I hate seeing this.

A friend I am eating pizza and calamari with asks me about my parents and about my childhood and all I can think to say is that I'm so thankful that I wanted to win running races. She says, I'm already feeling this wine.

My friend says, I'm doing some serious Japanese cleaning. The Japanese get cleaning, she says, they get how filthy people are.

I try to find a poem or a very short story I once wrote. I plug an old external drive into my laptop and think, there are so many files. I don't want to see all of these files, just the one I'm looking for. I know that in the poem or very short story I'm looking for there was an avocado, or maybe an avocado tree, and in one of the drafts I referred to a woman who either throws or eats an avocado as the neighbour.

Not feeling like myself

Not feeling like myself, I watch the first season of a television series about a man who moves with his family to a remote area with a lake to launder money, though he's already successfully laundering money in the city. The family buys a house they wouldn't otherwise be able to afford. There's no mention of renting. The reason they are able to afford the house is that it comes with the elderly previous owner named Buddy who says he'll die in a year or maybe a year and a half. I think, they couldn't stand the idea of filming the show in the type of house the family could afford so they came up with the elderly previous owner. I search for 'Buddy' on the Wikipedia page for the show and there are fourteen hits. At the end of the synopsis of fourth episode of season two, it says, 'Buddy's health declines, but he recovers.' But then, in the sixth episode of season two, 'Buddy dies in Wendy's car and Jonah uses Buddy's Rolodex to contact his friends.'

More to the point

This is how we think it happened.
For a moment she stood with her hands
on a long steel rail noticing or knowing
or feeling that certain things had more weight than
she did. We have it down to: rain, particular car and truck
models, people who speak quietly on television and the radio, headphones
she and other people sometimes wore that were the size of two crushed cans
the sequence of events, the white rattan ceiling fan that had been taken down
and just left there, the church facade she stood in front of that made her feel
ludicrous and light, with its near perfect symmetry
and its flatness
that was almost convex. We have her
saying 'the contents of the world' and 'no'
and 'yes'.

It's true, my partner says, the Japanese do get how filthy people are.

My partner's mother says to my partner that she needs a list of ten words that she mispronounces for a pronunciation course she has enrolled in. I don't know why, but later in the night while we're watching a news program, long after we've finished eating, my partner's mother says 'poem'. That's one for your list, my partner says.

New in the family

My brother has a newly broken hand
My sister has a newly born son
My mother has a new camera and a new book and a new chair

I say I'm going to go look at the herbs.
What, she says.
I'm going to go look at the herbs.
I thought you were going to say something else, she says.

On a podcast I'm listening to, a man says there were only eight shots fired but another man says, no, there had to be more. A third man says he thinks someone might have gotten to the first man.

A man on the radio is clapping

Afterword

I don't know how that happened is a series of interrelated, small and domestic poems that seek to work at that space between the sentence and the story, or that place between sentences. While at times the language breaks, or fragments (my first love was L=A=N=G=U=A=G=E, for the gaps, for better or worse) I am deeply interested in thinking about, and attempting to locate, where exactly abstraction takes place with words, in both poetry and prose, and whether abstraction, or just the conveyance of something not directly there, can be brought about through apparently simple, clear language.

I find the impossibility of the written still life to be generative, the impossibility of a trapped stillness, the way life can't help but slide or leach its way in, subsume (William Carlos Williams, Peter Balakian, Seamus Heaney of *Seeing Things*). David Hockney has spent many years considering the problem of translating the world into a flat panel. There is deep pleasure, I have found, in the works in any medium of those who capture or enact this translation precisely (and in whose work we see and feel the problems seen, acknowledged, met) but whose work also echoes out, suggests, tempts and leaches its way into us: Marie Howe's *Magdalene*, say.

As understated, or even slight, as this series of poems is or feels, I hope that they capture, that they echo.

Acknowledgements

Biggest and greatest and endless thanks to my partner Jess Au, for being an optimal human, but also for reading, critiquing, and for having inflexible standards. And also thanks to those people who have, over time, read my work, or whose work I have read, or who have been superb literary and non-literary or extra-literary conversationalists: Antonia Pont, Sean O'Beirne, Alice Bishop, Jo Case, Bel Monypenny, Anna Thwaites, Julia Prendergast, Em Kiddell, Jon Hopkins, Caitie Lawless, Maria Takolander, SJ Finn, Pania Walton, Amelia Dowe and, of course, all the Beeds: Lou Swinn, Eleanor Thomas, Miles Vertigan, Erin Richardson, Gus Treyvaud, Jodie Webster and Nicki Greenberg. And thank you to everyone who has, over the years, been involved in the *Slow Canoe*, for contributing to atmosphere and motion, to a kind of space. Thanks to Shane Strange and Recent Work Press for producing this book and other books so beautifully. And, finally, thanks to my parents, for being interesting, for being enthusiasts.

About the Author

Oliver Driscoll is a poet, essayist and short story writer, and a co-organiser of the *Slow Canoe* Live Journal and Press. Oliver grew up in North Queensland, and now lives in Melbourne, where he's a bookseller and sometimes sessional academic. I *don't know how that happened* is his debut collection.

www.ingramcontent.com/pod-product-compliance
Lightning Source LLC
Chambersburg PA
CBHW020330010526
44107CB00054B/2057